DINOS
STICKER ACTIVITY
BOOK

Pull out the sticker sheets and keep
them by you as you complete each page.
There are also lots of extra stickers to
use in this book or anywhere you want!
Have fun!

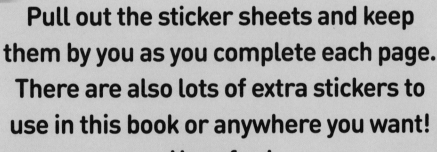
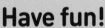

NATIONAL GEOGRAPHIC
Washington, D.C.

Consultant: Peter Ricketts
Editorial, Design, and Production by
make believe ideas

Picture credits: All dinosaur artwork by **Franco Tempesta/National Geographic** unless as follows: **DAMN FX/National Geographic Creative:** 35 tl; **John Sibbick/National Geographic Creative:** 36 tm (Pteranodon);
Make Believe Ideas: 1 tl; ml; mr, 2 tr, 2, 3 m (T. rex), 3 tl; ml; m; mr, 4 tm; mr; br, 5 br (branch), 6, 7 m (Diplodocus), 7 bl, 9 ml, 12 tr, 14 tl; mr, 15 tl; ml; mr; bl, 19 m, 20 mr, 24 ml; mr; bm; br, 25 tl; ml; br, 26 ml; mr;
maze images: Allosaurus x2: tr; m, 27 tr; ml, 29 tm; mr, 30 tl; bl; br, 31 mr (Parasaurolophus x3); bl, 33 mr (dragonfly); mr (butterfly), 34 tl, 34, 35 m (Kronosaurus), 36 tm; m (pterosaur x2); mr; bl (pterosaur x2); br,
36, 37 (background), 37 tm; mr; bm (pterosaur x3); bl (pterosaur); bl (ball); br (red pterosaur); br (seaweed); **Make Believe Ideas/Graham Kennedy:** 30 tm; ml; mr; **Shutterstock:** 3 bm (leaves x6); bm (eggs x2), 6 m,
8 tr (background), 14 bm (background); ml, 15 bm, 17 mr, 21 tm; tr, 24, 25 b (background), 26 maze images: Ceratosaurus x2: mr; bl, leaf: br, 33 mr (seeds), 36 bm; **Xing Lida/National Geographic Creative:** 33 bm.

Sticker pages: All dinosaur artwork by **Franco Tempesta/National Geographic** unless as follows: **John Sibbick/National Geographic Creative:** 12, 13 Oviraptor, 36, 37 Quetzalcoatlus, 40 Alamosaurus; Anchiceratops;
Dromiceiomimus; Troodon; **Make Believe Ideas:** 2, 3 Pteranodon x2; T. rex x4, 4, 5 bones x2; leaves x3 (combined); dinosaurs x4; birds x4, 6, 7 dinosaurs x7, 8, 9 Amargasaurus; Iguanodon, 10, 11 Pachycephalosaurus;
Dilophosaurus, 14, 15 dinosaurs x3; dinosaur skulls x2; teddy bear, 20, 21 Deinonychus, 22, 23 Ankylosaurus, 24, 25 horns x3; Triceratops skull (medium), 26, 27 Ankylosaurus x2; tangerine, 28, 29 4x4; school bus; igloo;
bed; Apatosaurus, 32, 33 ice cream; T-shirt, 36, 37 pterosaur; Pteranodon, 38, 39 skulls x2; skeleton; **Make Believe Ideas/Graham Kennedy:** 30, 31 Corythosaurus (matching activity); Saurolophus; Lambeosaurus;
Pixeldust Studios/National Geographic Creative: 10, 11 Carnotaurus, 16, 17 Masiakasaurus; **Raul Martin/National Geographic Creative:** 34, 35 Deinosuchus; **Shutterstock:** 2, 3 eggs x3, 4, 5 leaf x4,
24, 25 Triceratops skull (small) x2, 28, 29 boat; house; Argentinosaurus, 34, 35 Plesiosaurus; **Xing Lida/National Geographic Creative:** 32, 33 Caudipteryx; Microraptor x4.
Make Believe Ideas dinosaur images from products supplied by: www.dinosaurtime.co.uk.

What is a dinosaur?

Dinosaurs were animals that lived more than 65 million years ago.

Color T. rex's scaly skin!

Tyrannosaurus rex
tye-RAN-oh-SORE-us rex

Find the missing stickers to finish T. rex!

scaly skin

long tail

Pteranodon
teh-RAN-uh-don

Dinosaurs lived on land. Animals that flew or lived in the ocean are not called dinosaurs.

sharp teeth

Elasmosaurus
el-LAZ-moe-SORE-us

Dinosaurs hatched from eggs. Sticker more eggs!

claws

3

Meet the different dinos!

Dinosaurs were either lizard-hipped like Allosaurus or bird-hipped like Stegosaurus.

Allosaurus
AL-oh-SORE-us

Sticker the different hip bones onto the skeletons.

Stegosaurus
STEG-oh-SORE-us

Bird-hipped dinosaurs ate only plants.

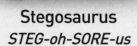

Sticker tasty plants for the dinosaur to eat.

Parasaurolophus
pa-ra-SORE-OH-lo-fus

BIRD-HIPPED

Triceratops
tri-SERR-ah-tops

Stegosaurus

Sticker the dinos to discover which group they belonged to.

LIZARD-HIPPED

T. rex

Brachiosaurus
BRACK-ee-oh-SORE-us

Some lizard-hipped dinosaurs are the ancestors of today's birds!

Color the dinosaur.

Sticker the birds!

Velociraptor   *vel-OSS-ee-rap-tor*

The age of the dinosaurs

Help the dino get through the maze to his friend!

Start

Dinosaurs lived through different time periods called the Triassic, Jurassic, and Cretaceous.

Finish

Sticker the dinosaurs on the time line to see when they lived!

Plateosaurus
PLAT-ee-oh-SORE-us

Coelophysis
seel-OH-fie-sis

Diplodocus
dih-PLOD-uh-kus

Stegosaurus

6

252 million years ago
Triassic

201 million years ag
Jurassic

Use the grid to draw the dino!

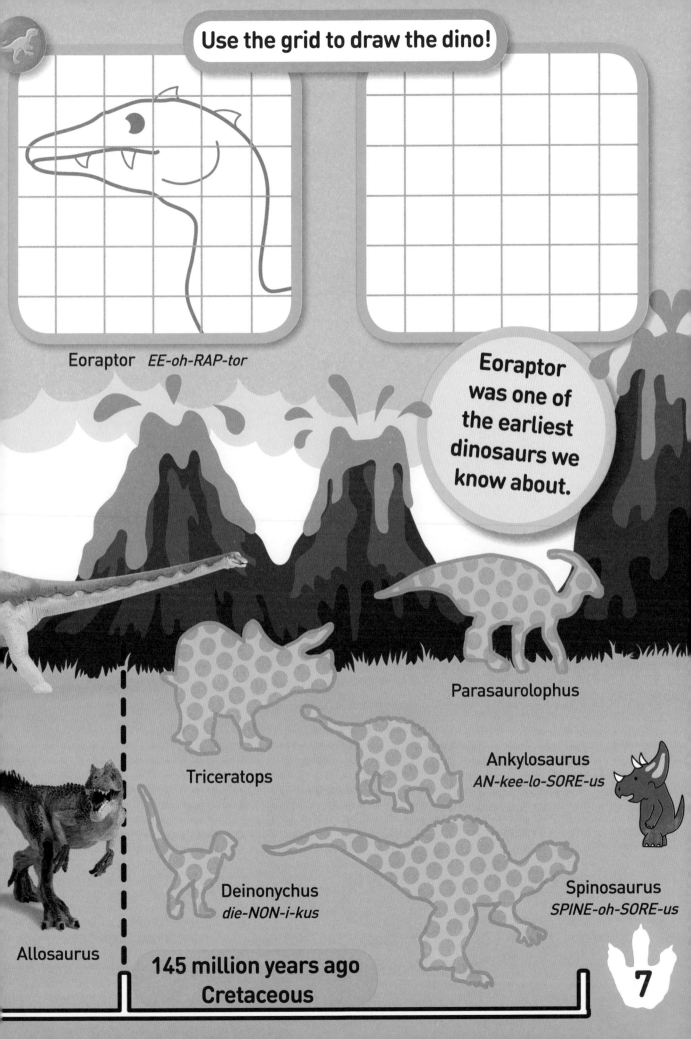

Eoraptor   *EE-oh-RAP-tor*

Eoraptor was one of the earliest dinosaurs we know about.

Parasaurolophus

Triceratops

Ankylosaurus
AN-kee-lo-SORE-us

Deinonychus
die-NON-i-kus

Spinosaurus
SPINE-oh-SORE-us

Allosaurus

**145 million years ago
Cretaceous**

7

Cool Triassic, Jurassic, and Cretaceous dinos

Coelophysis was a carnivore, which means it ate other animals.

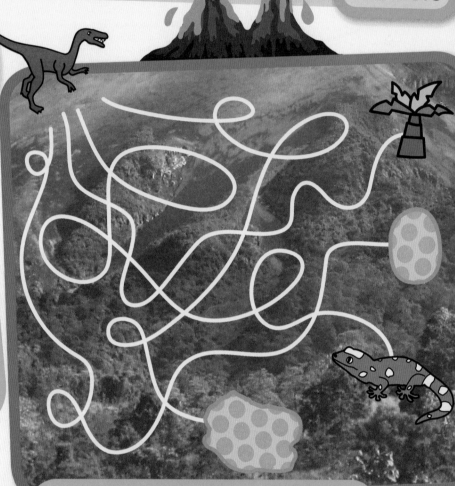

Coelophysis

Help Coelophysis find its food!

Herrerasaurus
huh-RARE-ah-SORE-us

Riojasaurus
REE-oh-hah-SORE-us

Finish the erupting volcano!

JURASSIC

Scientists used Archaeopteryx's fossils to discover that birds are related to dinosaurs.

Archaeopteryx
ARK-ee-OP-turr-icks

Yangchuanosaurus
YANG-chew-an-oh-SORE-us

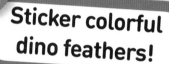

Sticker colorful dino feathers!

Brachiosaurus

CRETACEOUS

These Cretaceous dinosaurs were . . .

TINY!

Microraptor
MY-cro-RAP-tore

SPINY!

Amargasaurus
uh-MARG-uh-SORE-us

Find the missing stickers.

SPIKY!

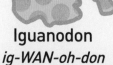

Iguanodon
ig-WAN-oh-don

FIERCE!

T. rex

FRILLY!

Triceratops

9

Weird and wonderful dinos

Find the missing stickers and color the picture frames!

Although Therizinosaurus's claws were about 28 inches (70 cm) long, it probably ate only plants!

Therizinosaurus
THERE-ih-ZIN-oh-SORE-us

Carnotaurus
KAR-no-TORE-us

Pachycephalosaurus had an ultra-thick skull!

Carnotaurus had really tiny arms!

Pachycephalosaurus
pack-ee-SEF-ah-lo-SORE-us

Draw a funny dinosaur face!

Ouranosaurus had super spines!

Ouranosaurus
oo-RAHN-oh-SORE-us

Shunosaurus
SHOO-noh-SORE-us

Shunosaurus had a cool club-tail!

Dilophosaurus
die-LOAF-oh-sore-us

Design your own cool crest using color and stickers!

Dilophosaurus had a crest on its head.

Baby dinos hatched from eggs!

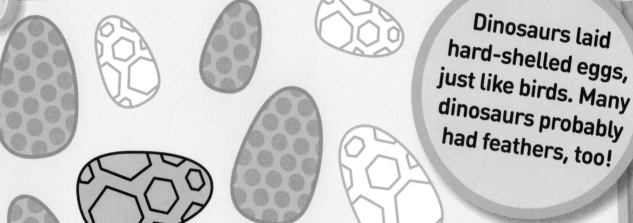

Dinosaurs laid hard-shelled eggs, just like birds. Many dinosaurs probably had feathers, too!

Color and sticker the eggs, then circle the one that's cracked!

Oviraptor
OH-vih-RAP-tore

Oviraptors built nests for their young.

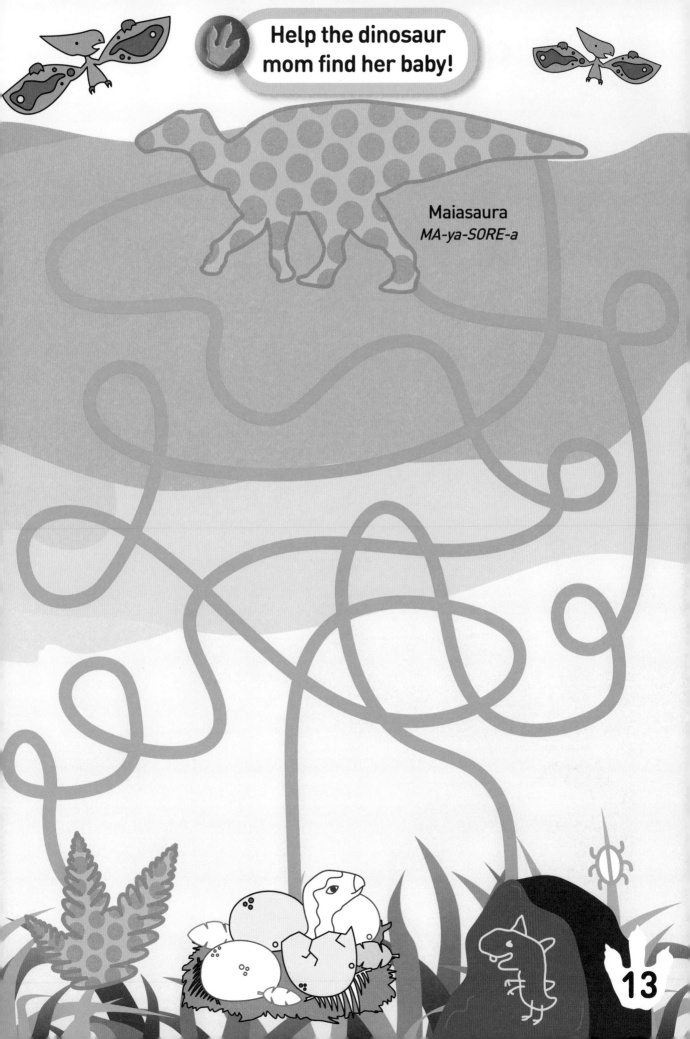

Help the dinosaur mom find her baby!

Maiasaura
MA-ya-SORE-a

13

Predators hunted other animals for food

Help Allosaurus find its meal!

Allosaurus was a meat-eater. Its sharp teeth were up to 4 inches (10 cm) long!

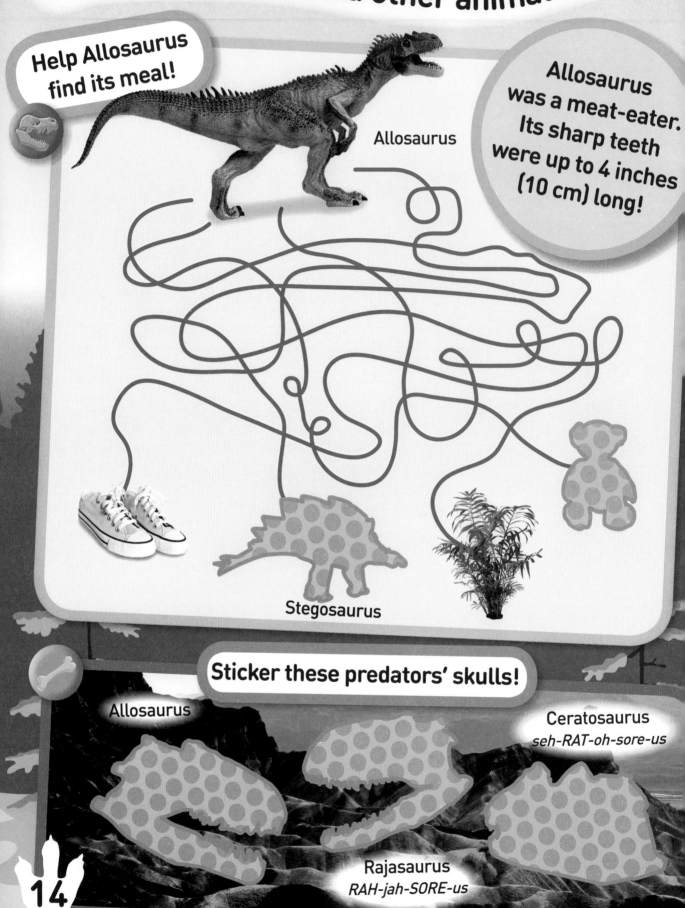

Allosaurus

Stegosaurus

Sticker these predators' skulls!

Allosaurus

Ceratosaurus
seh-RAT-oh-sore-us

Rajasaurus
RAH-jah-SORE-us

predator

T. rex

prey

fish

Predators are animals that chase and kill other animals. The animals they kill are their prey.

prey

Triceratops

predator

Spinosaurus

The tiny meat-eater Compsognathus was only as big as a turkey!

Compsognathus
KOMP-sog-NAH-thus

Color Compsognathus hiding in the bushes.

Deinonychus

Sticker more meat-eaters!

Tenontosaurus
ten-ON-toe-SORE-us

15

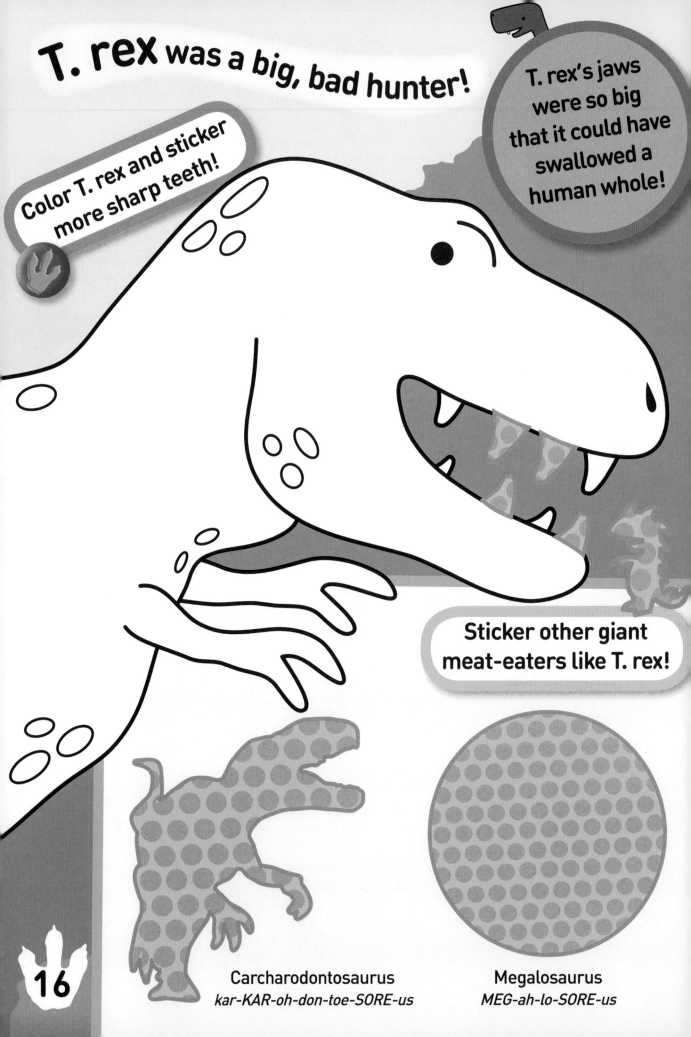

T. rex was a big, bad hunter!

T. rex's jaws were so big that it could have swallowed a human whole!

Color T. rex and sticker more sharp teeth!

Sticker other giant meat-eaters like T. rex!

16

Carcharodontosaurus
kar-KAR-oh-don-toe-SORE-us

Megalosaurus
MEG-ah-lo-SORE-us

T. rex's arms weren't long enough to reach its mouth!

Give the dinosaur amazing arms, then decorate it with stickers and color.

T. rex

Giganotosaurus
gig-an-OH-toe-SORE-us

Masiakasaurus
mash-YUCK-uh-SORE-us

17

Spinosaurus and Baryonyx
were fierce fish-eaters!

Spinosaurus and Baryonyx had sharp teeth and hook-like claws to grab fish!

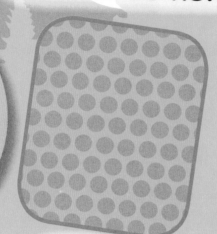

Baryonyx
bah-ree-ON-icks

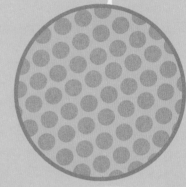

Spinosaurus

Find out who will reach the fishy dinner!

Spinosaurus could grow to about 50 feet (15.2 m) long, and its spines were at least 5 feet (1.5 m) tall!

Color the amazing spines!

Sticker and color more fish for Spinosaurus.

19

Velociraptor and Deinonychus were speedy predators!

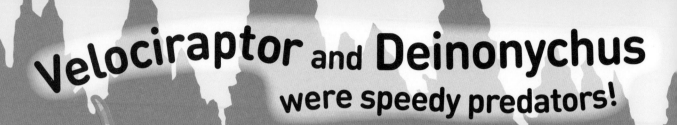

Help Deinonychus find its prey.

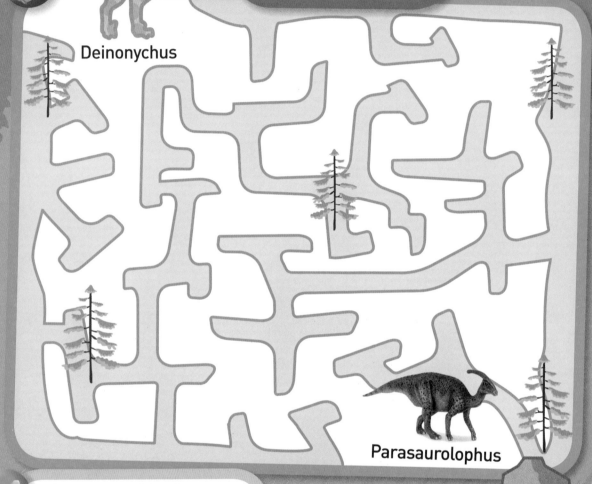

Deinonychus

Parasaurolophus

Connect the dots to discover Deinonychus!

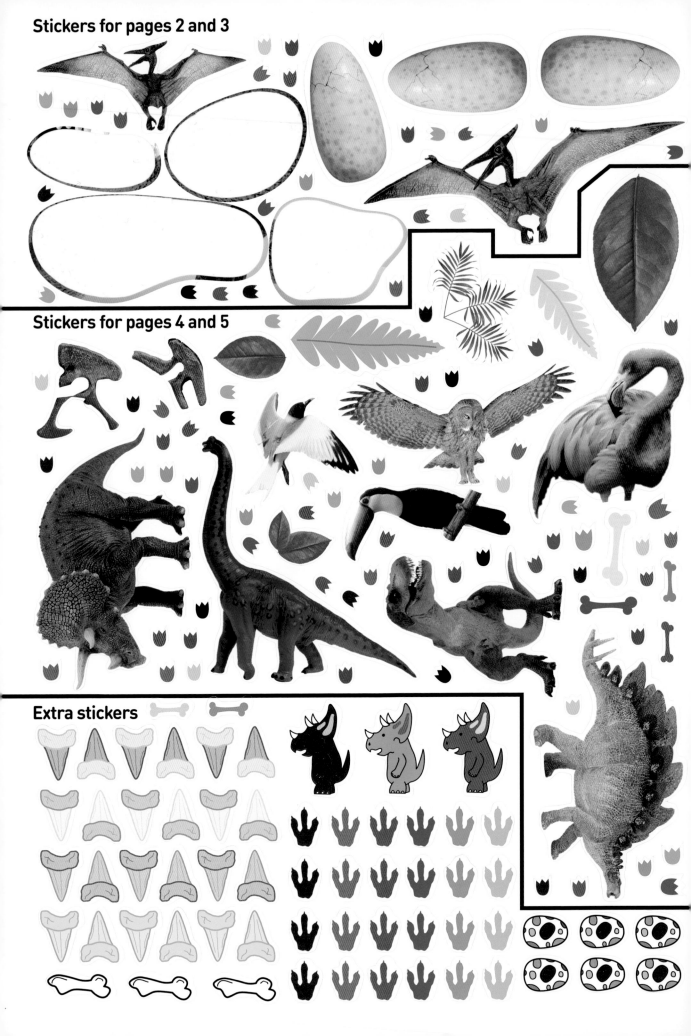

Stickers for pages 2 and 3

Stickers for pages 4 and 5

Extra stickers

Stickers for pages 6 and 7

Stickers for pages 8 and 9

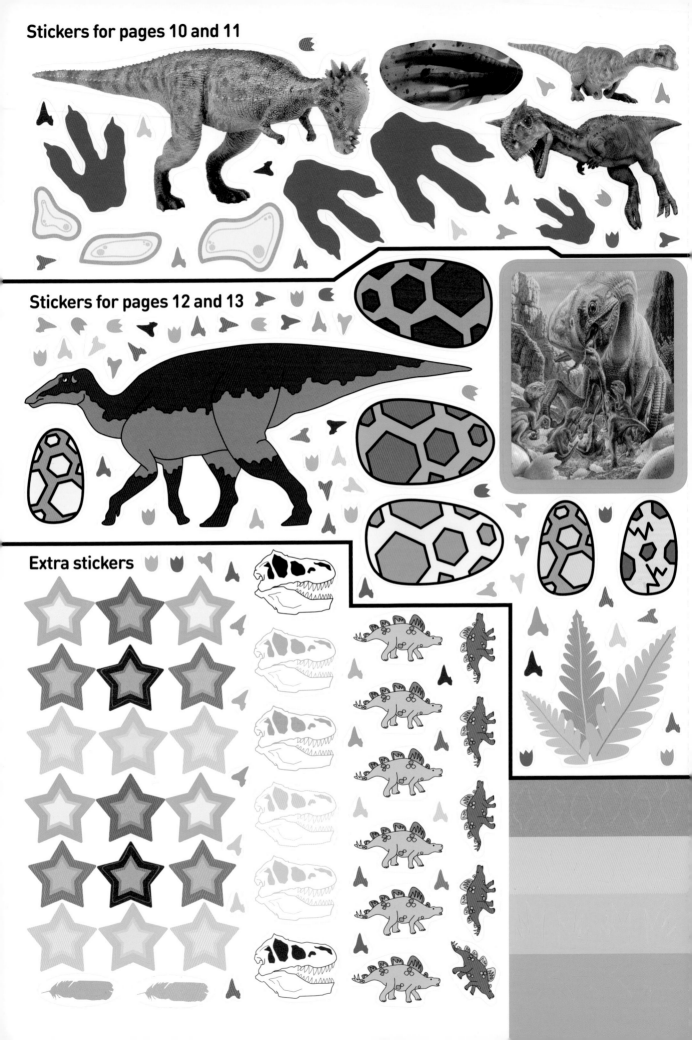

Stickers for pages 10 and 11

Stickers for pages 12 and 13

Extra stickers

Stickers for pages 14 and 15

Stickers for pages 16 and 17

Stickers for pages 18 and 19

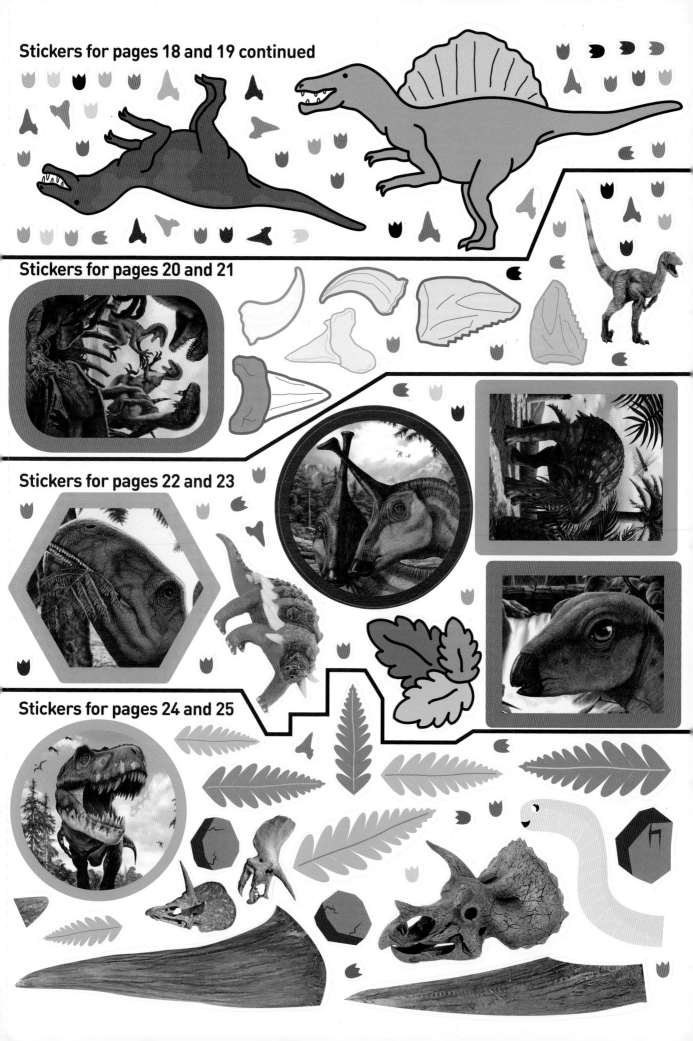

Stickers for pages 18 and 19 continued

Stickers for pages 20 and 21

Stickers for pages 22 and 23

Stickers for pages 24 and 25

Stickers for pages 26 and 27

Stickers for pages 28 and 29

Stickers for pages 30 and 31

Extra stickers

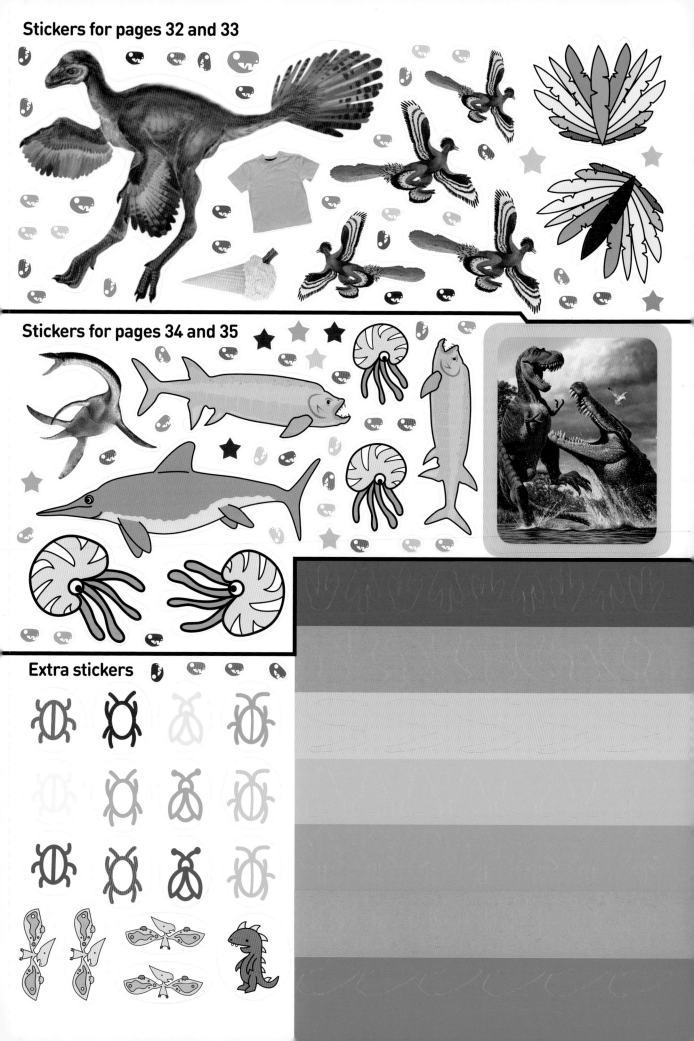

Stickers for pages 32 and 33

Stickers for pages 34 and 35

Extra stickers

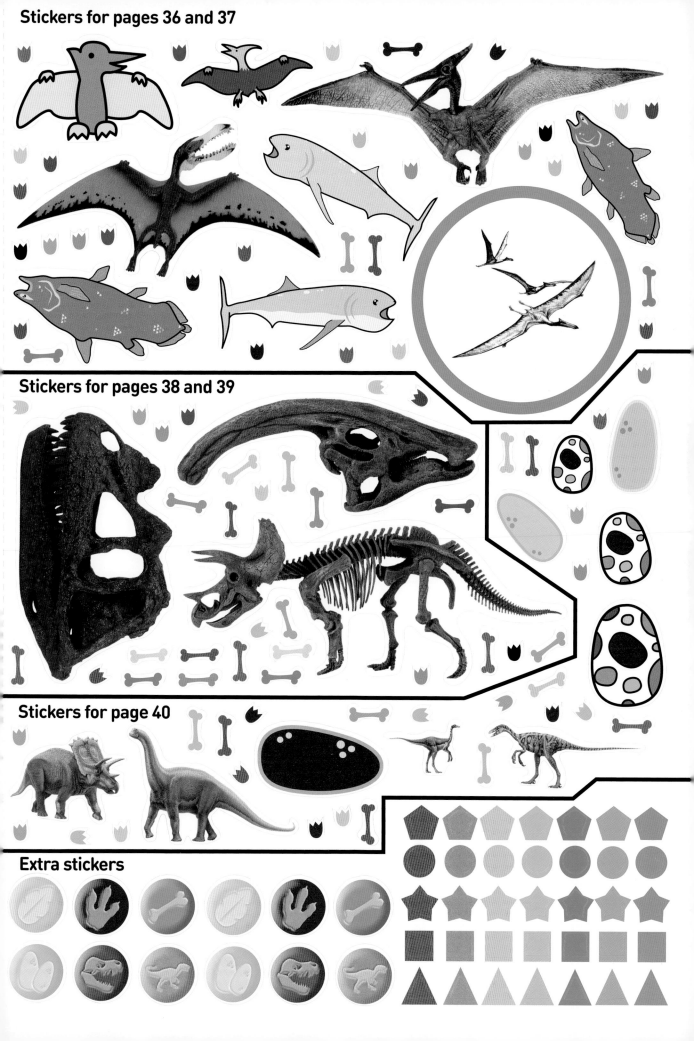

Stickers for pages 36 and 37

Stickers for pages 38 and 39

Stickers for page 40

Extra stickers

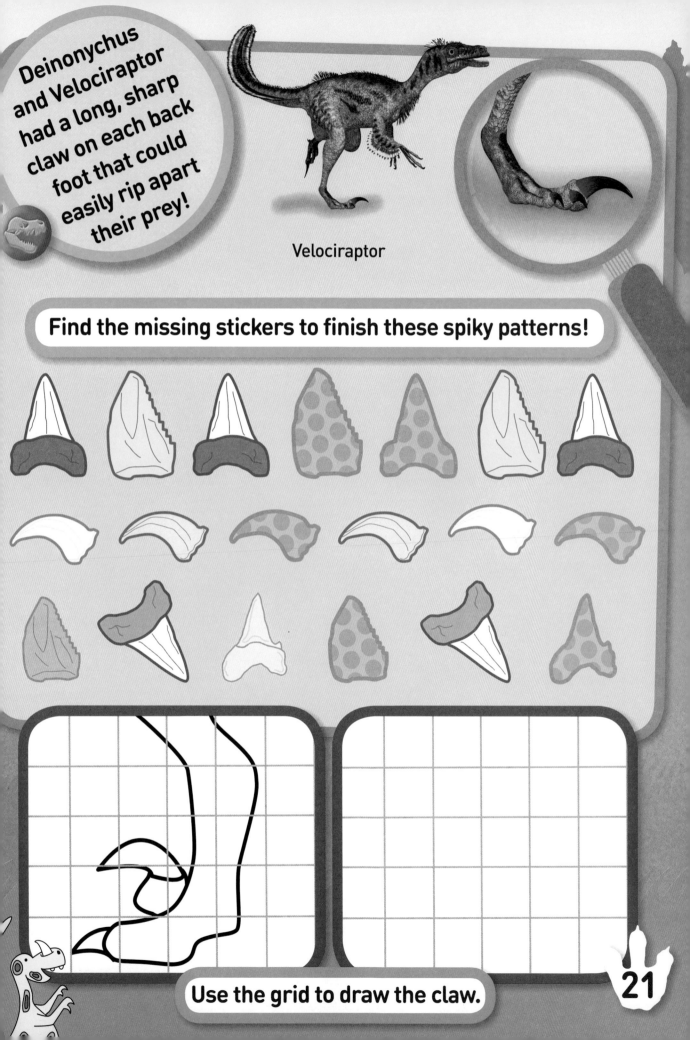

Deinonychus and Velociraptor had a long, sharp claw on each back foot that could easily rip apart their prey!

Velociraptor

Find the missing stickers to finish these spiky patterns!

Use the grid to draw the claw.

21

Herbivores were plant-eating dinos!

Connect the dots to find Ankylosaurus, then add color.

Ankylosaurus had to eat a huge amount of plants to feed itself—and probably produced a lot of gas as a result!

Ankylosaurus

Brachiosaurus

Color Brachiosaurus!

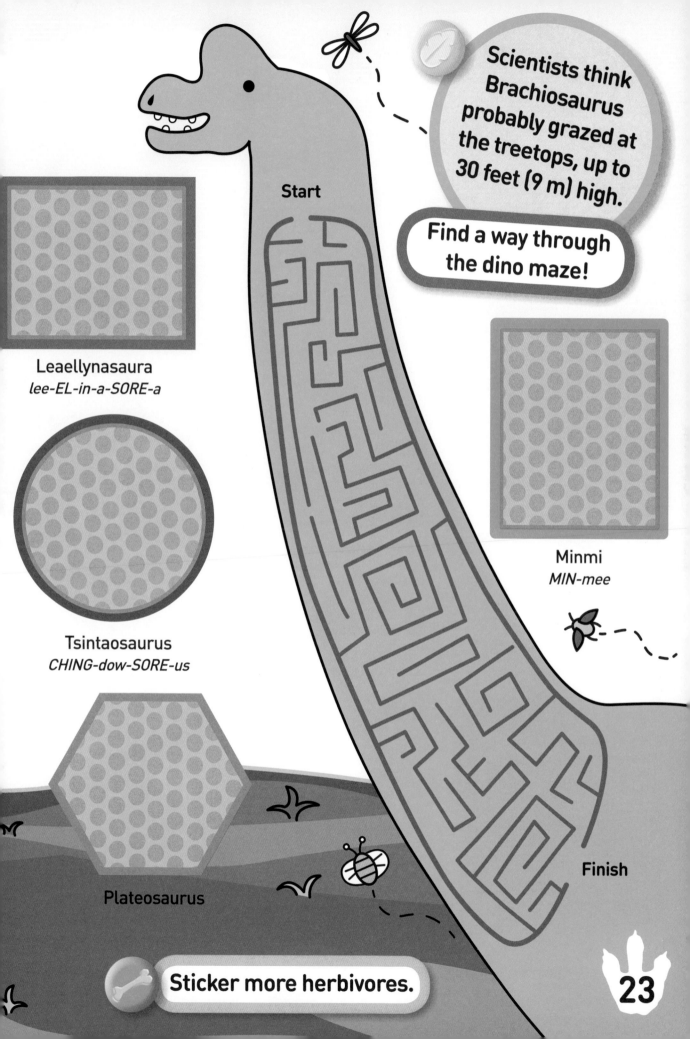

Start

Scientists think Brachiosaurus probably grazed at the treetops, up to 30 feet (9 m) high.

Find a way through the dino maze!

Leaellynasaura
lee-EL-in-a-SORE-a

Minmi
MIN-mee

Tsintaosaurus
CHING-dow-SORE-us

Finish

Plateosaurus

Sticker more herbivores.

23

Triceratops means three-horned face!

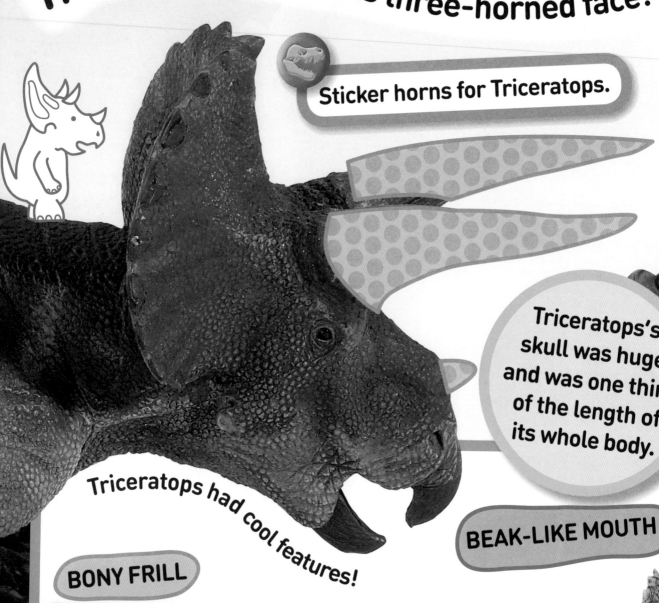

Sticker horns for Triceratops.

Triceratops's skull was huge and was one third of the length of its whole body.

Triceratops had cool features!

BEAK-LIKE MOUTH

BONY FRILL

Sticker more plants for Triceratops to eat.

Amazing armored dinosaurs

Stegosaurus had huge bony plates and tail spikes!

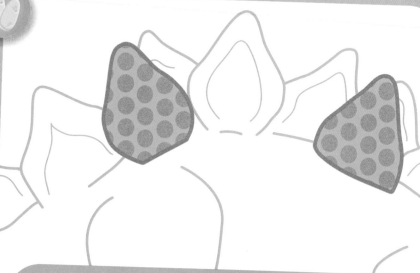

Sticker and color Stegosaurus's plates.

Start

Finish

Ankylosaurus's belly was the only part of its body not covered in armor!

Help Stegosaurus reach its food without running into Allosaurus or Ceratosaurus.

With its club-tail, Ankylosaurus was ready for battle!

Find the missing stickers to armor Ankylosaurus!

Stegosaurus's brain was only about the size of a tangerine!

Use the grid to draw the dino.

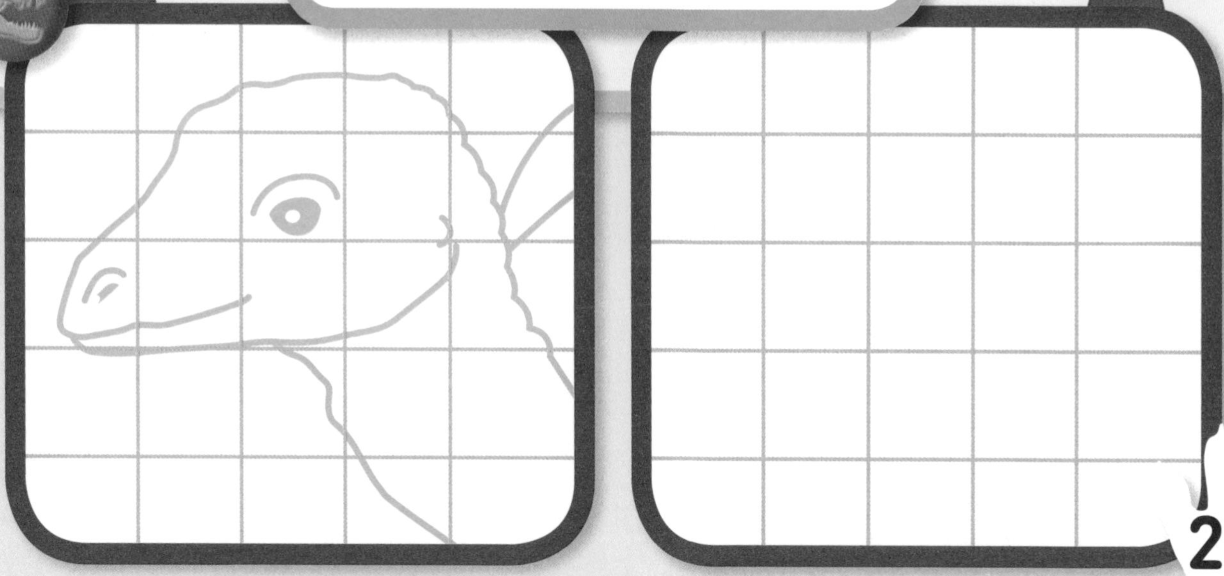

Stegosaurus

27

Giant sauropods had **long necks!**

Sticker more leaves for these sauropod dinosaurs.

Sauropods were massive, plant-eating dinosaurs. They had enormous bodies, but their heads were tiny!

Give these dinosaurs colorful, long necks!

Find more giant sauropods!

Sticker everyday objects to show how big these beasts were!

Mamenchisaurus
mah-MEHN-chee-SORE-us

Argentinosaurus
arh-gen-TEEN-oh-SORE-us

Mamenchisaurus and Argentinosaurus were two of the biggest dinosaurs in the world!

Diplodocus

Sticker more dinosaur footprints!

Apatosaurus
uh-PAT-uh-SORE-us

You could take a bath in one of Diplodocus's footprints!

29

Discover **duck-billed** dinos!

Sticker the duck-billed dinos and draw lines to match the pairs.

Parasaurolophus

Saurolophus
SORE-oh-LOAF-us

Lambeosaurus
LAM-bee-oh-SORE-us

Corythosaurus
co-RITH-oh-SORE-us

HONK!

Parasaurolophus may have made honking sounds using the crest on its head!

Sticker a colorful song for these noisy dinosaurs!

Corythosaurus

Draw yourself riding on a Parasaurolophus!

Edmontosaurus
ed-MON-toh-SORE-us

Humans have up to 32 teeth, but some duck-billed dinosaurs had up to 1,500!

Finish

Start

Help Mother Parasaurolophus find her three babies!

Fun, feathered dinosaurs

Make the feathers bright and colorful!

Caudipteryx
caw-DIP-turr-iks

Caudipteryx had a feathery tail and was the size of a peacock. Scientists cannot agree whether it was a dinosaur or a bird!

Find the missing stickers, then find which tail is different.

Draw the other half of the tail.

Help Caudipteryx find seeds and insects to eat!

Microraptor was another feathered dinosaur. It even had feathers on its back legs!

Microraptor

Sticker some friends for Microraptor!

33

Incredible creatures filled the oceans!

These amazing creatures lived in or near water. They were not dinosaurs.

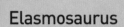

Elasmosaurus

Plesiosaurus
plee-zee-oh-SORE-us

Finish

Start

Help Plesiosaurus swim through the sea without hitting any rocks or fish!

Ticinosuchus
tih-SEEN-oh-SOO-kus

Deinosuchus
die-no-SOO-kus

Ticinosuchus was a small, powerful predator that hunted the swamps for its prey.

Deinosuchus was a giant crocodile. It grew up to 36 feet (11 m) long!

Kronosaurus
KRON-oh-SORE-us

Ichthyosaurus
IK-thee-oh-SORE-us

Liopleurodon
LIE-oh-PLOO-ro-don

Color Liopleurodon!

35

Pterosaurs roamed the skies.

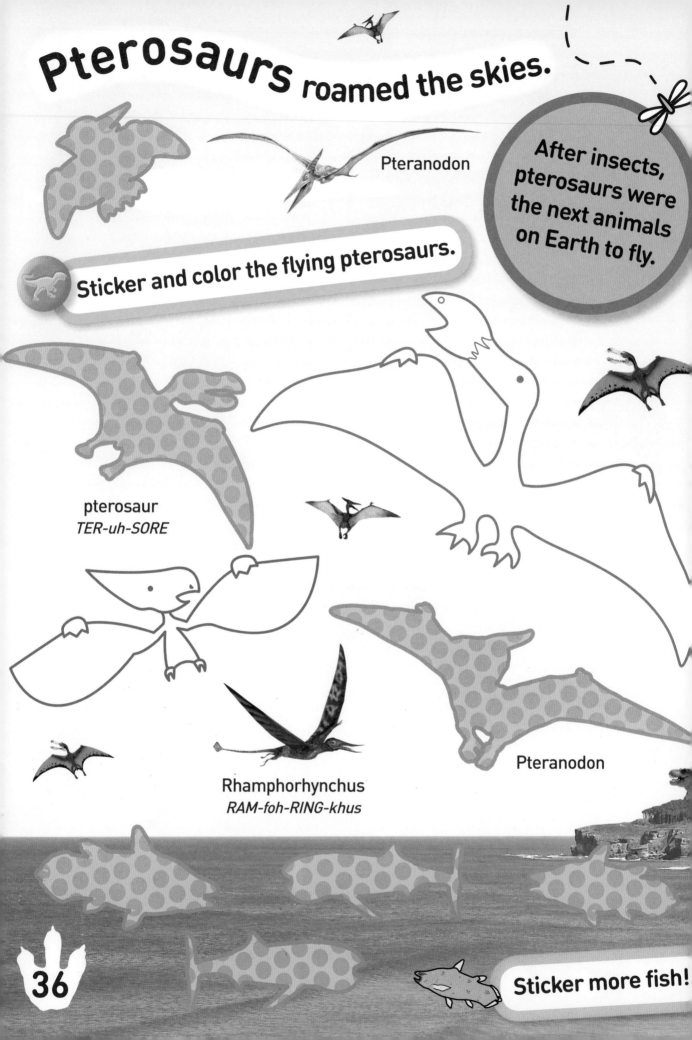

Pteranodon

After insects, pterosaurs were the next animals on Earth to fly.

Sticker and color the flying pterosaurs.

pterosaur
TER-uh-SORE

Rhamphorhynchus
RAM-foh-RING-khus

Pteranodon

Sticker more fish!

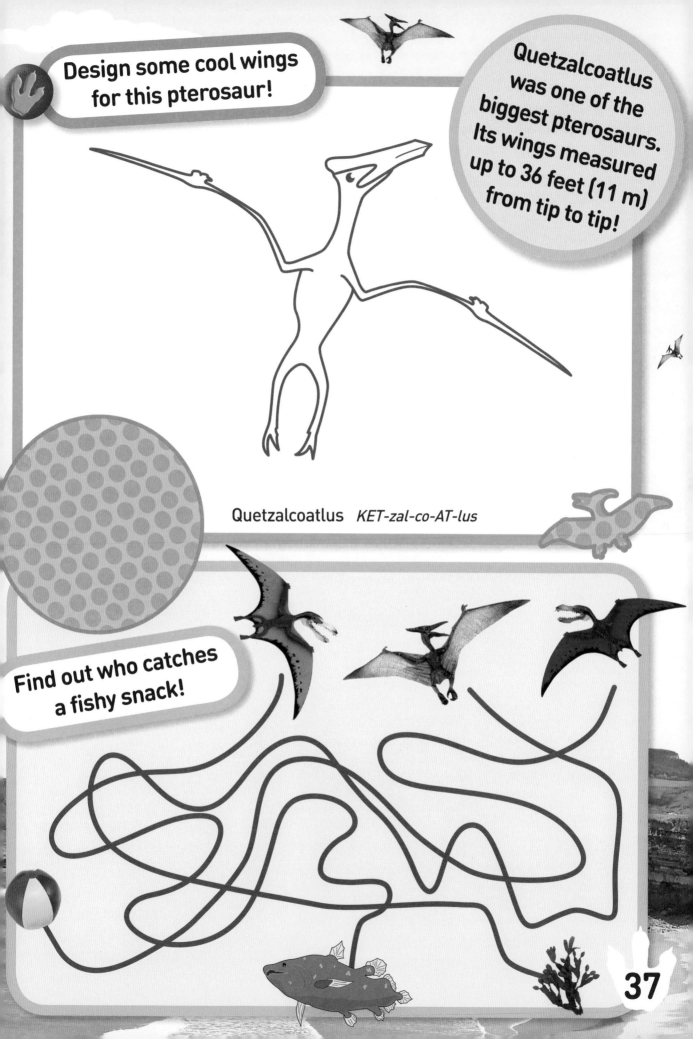

Design some cool wings for this pterosaur!

Quetzalcoatlus was one of the biggest pterosaurs. Its wings measured up to 36 feet (11 m) from tip to tip!

Quetzalcoatlus   *KET-zal-co-AT-lus*

Find out who catches a fishy snack!

Be a **fossil** hunter!

Connect the dots to discover the fossil!

We know about dinosaurs from the fossils of their bones and teeth, which are often found in rocks.

Use the grid to draw the fossil!

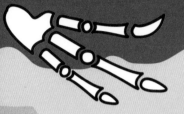

Find six hidden blue teeth fossils.

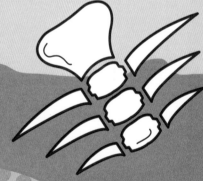

My favorite **dinos!**

Color the dinosaurs!

Connect the dots!

Draw an awesome dino!

Sticker the dinosaurs!